COUNT OF TEN SAY AMEN

Learn To Pray in 10 Steps Before Bedtime

By Dr. Harry Assad Salem III

Illustrations by Kay Horn

Unless otherwise indicated, all Scripture quotations are taken from the *King James® Bible and the English Standard® Bible.* Copyright © 1982 by Thomas Nelson, Inc. Used by permission.

LEARNING PALS COUNT OF TEN SAY AMEN
ISBN 1-890370-39-8

Copyright © 2017 by Salem Family Ministries

Salem Family Ministries
PO Box 1595
Cathedral City, CA 92234
www.salemfamilyministries.org

No part of this book may be reproduced or transmitted in any form or by any means, electronic or mechanical, including photocopying, recording, or by any information storage and retrieval system, without permission in writing from Salem Family Ministries.

Disclaimer: The views expressed in this book contain personal opinions, theories, and experiences throughout life and time spent in God's word and private research. They are expressed as opinion and views only, and are shared with you from lifelong experience and research. They are only communicated to you through what has been revealed from personal study and research.

-INTRODUCTION-

"TEACHING KIDS TO PRAY

It is important to teach children how to pray. It is vital that they learn to pray correctly. Communication with God is the key to building a solid foundation of faith and relationship with God. In the following pages we will show young people how easy it is to pray in ten easy steps. Each count from one to ten will help teach each child what to do, say, and think about as they pray. Saying the prayer at bedtime helps the child to get into a routine of praying at a certain time and remembering all the steps they were taught to pray. Praying before bed will also help each boy and girl who prays have a better night's sleep as they keep themselves in God's thoughts after talking to Him just before they lay their heads down to rest. Psalm 4:8 ESV says, *"In peace I will both lie down and sleep; for you alone, O Lord, make me dwell in safety."* Now let's have fun and teach our children how to pray.

God loves to talk to us.

God loves when we talk to Him.

How do we talk to God?

We talk to Him through prayer.

Let's learn to pray
by the count of ten.

Ready and set, now here we go!

Count of one,
we get on our knees.

Count of two,
we close our eyes.

Count of three,
we bow our heads.

Count of four,
we say, "Dear God."

Count of five,
we ask God to
bless those we love.

Count of six,
we say we are sorry for
our sins, which are
things that make God sad.

Count of seven,
we ask God for
a good night's sleep
and happy dreams.

Count of eight,
we say, "Thank you, God,
for hearing our prayers."

Count of nine,
we say,
"In Jesus' name."

Count of ten,
we say, "Amen."

With our prayers done
we are ready for bed
and say, "Goodnight."

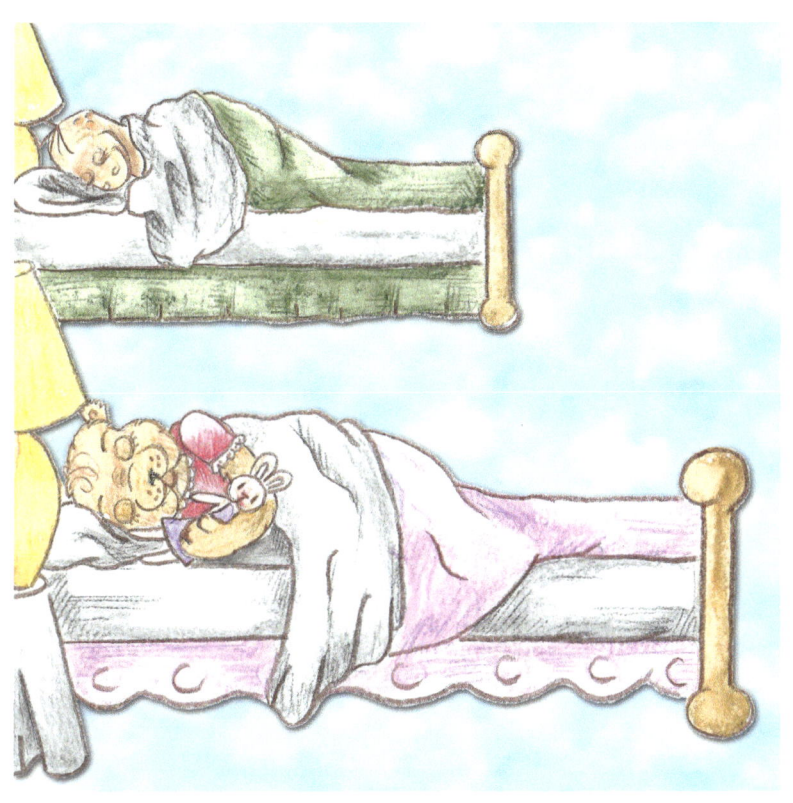

CLOSING AND GRATITUDE

Thanks to all of you for reading. I hope that you enjoyed learning how to pray and talk to God. It is always good to communicate with our Heavenly Father so we can be close to Him. It is also important to learn how to do new things in life. I hope that by learning how to pray that you will want to continue learning and enjoying everything that the wonderful world God has created has to offer. Blessings and prosperity to all of you.

ABOUT THE AUTHOR

Dr. Harry Assad Salem III is an author of several books dealing with theology, archaeology, religion, history, and science. He holds state, regional, national, and world championships and titles in the sports of powerlifting and strongman.

Dr. Salem holds five doctorate degrees in the fields of theology, archaeology, Biblical studies, Christian education, and practical ministry. He has been involved in ministry since the age of thirteen with Salem Family Ministries. He has lectured at School of Worship for several years. He has developed an children's book series called Prayer Buddies with two books already published with book one *Count of Ten Say Amen* and *Ten Steps to Build and be Spirit Filled.*

Dr. Salem is an advocate of education who believes that the highest goals one can achieve can be reached through knowledge and skills learned in a classroom, on the job, and then applied in the world to gain experience and mastery of anything and everything taught. Dr. Salem's personal motto and creed "Excellence is Excellent" is a belief that has kept him thriving for the highest of excellence in every life pursuit he has worked towards. He hopes to inspire others to achieve their own pursuits of excellence, foster climates of change in their lives, and live life to their fullest potential in anyway and everyway possible. He has one niece, Mia Gabrielle Salem, and one nephew, Roman Harry Salem Jr.

I would love to hear from you. There are many ways to stay connected to me. You can contact me either through the mail or the internet at the ministry website.

Salem Family Ministries

P.O. Box 1595

Cathedral City, CA 92234

www.salemfamilyministries.org

www.ingramcontent.com/pod-product-compliance
Lightning Source LLC
Chambersburg PA
CBHW041528090426
42736CB00036B/238